The Intuitive Arts
on
FAMILY

The Intuitive Arts
on
FAMILY

Arlene Tognetti and Cathy Jewell

ALPHA

A member of Penguin Group (USA) Inc.

International Standard Book Number: 1-59257-110-7
Library of Congress Catalog Card Number: 2003110650

05   04   03   8   7   6   5   4   3   2   1

Interpretation of the printing code: The rightmost number of the first series of numbers is the year of the book's printing; the rightmost number of the second series of numbers is the number of the book's printing. For example, a printing code of 03-1 shows that the first printing occurred in 2003.

Printed in the United States of America

Publisher: Marie Butler-Knight
Product Manager: Phil Kitchel
Senior Managing Editor: Jennifer Chisholm
Senior Acquisitions Editor: Randy Ladenheim-Gil
Book Producer: Lee Ann Chearney/Amaranth Illuminare
Development Editor: Lynn Northrup
Senior Production Editor: Christy Wagner
Copy Editor: Keith Cline
Technical Editor: Reba Jean Cain
Cover Designer: Charis Santillie
Book Designer: Trina Wurst
Creative Director: Robin Lasek
Layout/Proofreading: Angela Calvert, John Etchison

Contents

Introduction

Claim your brightest destiny and fulfill your own essential nature.

More than ever, we are searching for an inner awareness that brings outer confidence, joy, and direction. *The Intuitive Arts* series, with volumes on *Family, Health, Love, Money,* and *Work,* gives readers looking for answers to questions of daily living tools from the esoteric arts that help them look deeply, see, and make real changes affecting their futures. In each problem-solving volume, curious querents are presented exercises in the Intuitive Arts of Astrology, Tarot, and Psychic Intuition that examine, instruct, illuminate, and guide. In essence, you get three books for one—but also so much more!

An understanding of the interplay of the Intuitive Arts of Astrology, Tarot, and Psychic Intuition is something most people gain slowly over time, or with the aid of a professional Intuitive Arts practitioner who already has the knowledge to give in-depth readings that link the arts together.

In *The Intuitive Arts* series, expert author Arlene Tognetti shares her deep knowing of the arts of Astrology, Tarot, and Psychic Intuition to give you the best opportunity to work out solutions to life's problems and challenges with the benefit of the sophisticated relationships between the arts Arlene reveals chapter by chapter. By combining the Intuitive Arts together throughout each chapter's exercises, you'll gain insights that link the arts together—how, for example, Astrology's Moon ☽ signs are personified in Tarot cards that represent family archetypes. Or use your Psychic Intuition to create a family mandala harnessing the power of your Elemental Family Signature.

Arlene Tognetti and New Age book producer Lee Ann Chearney at Amaranth Illuminare created this series for Alpha Books to respond to the public's growing fascination with all things spiritual. People (like you!) want to know how they can use the Intuitive Arts to solve everyday challenges, plan for the future, and live in the present, with hands-on advice and techniques that will make things better for them. We want to help you improve the issues surrounding your unique life situation by providing a multi-art approach that gives you multiple pathways to personal growth and answers your questions about family, health, love, money, and work.

Using Tarot's Major and Minor Arcana cards and spreads; Astrology's birth charts and aspect grids, sign, planets, and houses; and Psychic Intuition's meditations, affirmations, and inner knowing exercises, the innovative *Intuitive Arts* series provides a truly interactive, solution-oriented, positive message that enriches a personal synergy of mind, body, and spirit!

Read on to further your knowledge and understanding of how the Intuitive Arts work together to reveal deep insights. In this series volume, *The Intuitive Arts on Family,* learn how Astrology, the Tarot, and Psychic Intuition reveal your future family harmony through the generations!

Are *you* ready to manifest the family that nurtures and inspires you?

chapter 1

Father and Mother, Sister and Brother

What are the Intuitive Arts?
Shining stars: Family and Astrology
It's all in the cards: Family and Tarot
What do your instincts say? Family and Psychic Intuition
Your family tree (or shrub, or garden)
What's next?

Singer-songwriter James Taylor may have had it right in a song his fans love, "Shower the People." When you give love to the people you care about most—your family—conditions can only improve and love increase. Every family has its joys and challenges, and this chapter explores the nature of family bonds, from a psychological and social viewpoint, in popular culture (past and present), and through the lens of the Intuitive Arts: Astrology, Tarot, and Psychic Intuition. What are these Intuitive Arts, and how do they look into and reveal how family shapes our lives? Let's find out!

What Are the Intuitive Arts?

Why did you pick up this book? Maybe you're already interested in the Intuitive Arts. You might have some family relationships you want to work on, or perhaps you're trying to create your own family. Whatever your place, we think the Intuitive Arts can help you get where you want to go. When we speak of the Intuitive Arts in this book, we mean these three practices: Astrology, Tarot, and Psychic Intuition. Each of these areas requires something of you: You learn the basic concepts of Astrology, and you need to have your astrological birth chart in hand; for the study of Tarot, you need your own Tarot deck; and for Psychic Intuition, all you need is your open mind.

Shining Stars: Family and Astrology

Astrology studies the heavens—the stars and planets. It is a quite complex and ancient science; we simplify some of its main concepts in this chapter. We use birth or natal charts throughout this book. A birth chart is a map of the heavens at the time of your birth—if you know your exact time of birth, this chart is very specific to you; if you don't, not to worry—many people have this problem. If you can't narrow your time of birth down at all, an astrologer will use noon on the day of your birth as your birth time. When we use noon as the birth time in this book, the chart is labeled a noon birth chart rather than simply a birth chart, to distinguish the two. What else does an astrologer need, besides your time of birth? The obvious, of course: the day, month, and year of your birth. The place of your birth is necessary, as well. You may want to collect some of this information for yourself and your family members now, so that you can have birth charts done—this will be very useful in some of the exercises we do in later chapters.

Arlene used the computer software program Solar Fire 5, published by Astrolabe, Inc., to generate the birth charts we've adapted as examples throughout this book. Charts are cast using the Geocentric view, Tropical Zodiac, Placidus house system, and True Node because these are the most common in modern Western Astrology. To use your birth chart with this book, you need to be sure to specify these parameters when generating your own astrological birth chart. You can order a birth chart online or from your local metaphysical bookstore; there's more information on how to order a birth chart in Appendix A at the back of this book. We've provided a sample birth chart with highlighted family connections in Appendix A, as well.

The Zodiac

You probably know your own Sun ☉ sign: This is determined by the position of the Sun when you were born. The path the Earth follows in its orbit around the Sun is called the *Zodiac*. There are 12 signs of the Zodiac, indicating the position of the Sun during the Earth's orbit; we've included a *Zodiac wheel*, so you can find your Sun sign (if you don't already know it) simply by finding your birthday.

Arlene recently did this spread for Cathy. What lessons is she learning right now? Here is Cathy's Karma Spread:

Cathy's Karma Spread.

Ace of Pentacles. This card signals the beginning of prosperity. Cathy is developing a good financial foundation, and she may also be looking toward new career ideas. Cathy will be learning to take care of new business offers or proposals coming into her life. She will learn to juggle her family life and her career life well!

3 of Wands. Being established in business, and pride in accomplishments. Cathy will be working toward goals she has looked forward to over the years. The 3 of Wands relates the energy she will have to accomplish those goals. She, like the fellow in the 3 of Wands, is looking upon the world and what she has already accomplished. Her karmic duty now is to continue on that course she has set in motion. Stay focused, and keep your eye on the prize!

Page of Wands. Good news and enthusiasm for life—adventure. The Page of Wands can be messages coming in for Cathy about work, home, or a positive nod toward a desire she has put much energy into. This page can also indicate that a new child may join her family. Cathy's karmic lessons can be through children and it looks as though (because the card is upright) she will have growth and great benefit through children. Arlene would say that a child or children to come are Cathy's karmic lessons and karmic rewards.

8 of Swords. Fear. This card indicates that fear is holding Cathy back—notice that the swords surround the woman but don't touch her, and she's bound and blindfolded. She's being kept in a difficult place because of fear. Cathy will need to release fear or worry about goals and dreams. The 8 of Swords is a woman who has been bound to fears not from the outside world but from her inner self. Cathy can release these fears or worries or anticipation of negative things. All Minor Arcana cards are open to change from our own free will. In other words, if Cathy wants to release this fear, she can! Then things will turn around. Cathy needs to breathe (Air is the Element of Swords!), relax, and meditate on what is holding her back.

Want to see what your life lessons are right now? Do your own reading and record your impressions in your Intuitive Arts notebook. Remember that, whatever the cards say, you don't have to be stuck repeating yourself and learning the same lessons over and over for your entire life—you can learn these karmic lessons and move on!

Karmic Lessons in Family

Now that you've done a Tarot spread to look at what your karmic lessons might be, we're going to look at some of the planets in your birth chart, and see what they can show you about the lessons you have to learn in this life, and how your lessons and those of your family members interrelate and overlap. It's back to the idea of past lives—we think we're connected to the people we know now for a reason: These people are helping us through our karmic lessons so that we can move into a higher state of being and awareness. Wouldn't it be great if, the next time around, you're one of those people completely unbothered by traffic jams? Or if you're open enough with yourself and others to have satisfying and harmonious family relationships? We think so. Of course, this doesn't just depend on how you deal with your own life lessons, but how others do this as well. Let's see how you can help yourself—and your family members—recognize and work through life's lessons productively.

More About Moon ☽ Signs

We went through the Moon ☽ signs in Chapter 6, and talked about our emotional compatibility with family members. We want to add that the Moon is the planet of memory and of past habits. It's the second most important planet in your birth chart (after the Sun ☉), and if the Sun can be looked at as your self (ego, individuality), the Moon is your soul (emotional needs and responses). The Moon also represents family, whether your family of origin or the family you have created for yourself, and it can relate to motherhood and nurturing, both your experience and expectations of nurturance. The Moon is the planet symbolically associated with Mother, family, Mother Nature, and the nurturing female influence. When the Moon is conjunct ☌ any of the personal planets (Sun ☉, Mercury ☿, Venus ♀, Mars ♂, or the ascendant), you take things to heart. You would be attached to the energy very strongly and be moved to react accordingly. When the Moon is conjunct ☌ the outer planets (Jupiter ♃, Saturn ♄, Uranus ♅, Neptune ♆, and Pluto ♇), you will attach yourself to the public's energy or may need the larger group to fulfill your emotional needs.

Saturn ♄: The Great Teacher

We looked at Saturn ♄ returns in Chapter 7, and we considered the kinds of lessons Saturn returns bring with them. Saturn returns make us reevaluate our lives, particularly in areas of responsibility and self-discipline. If you look at your birth chart, Saturn's placement—and particularly the sign it's in—will tell you what responsibilities will challenge you in life, as well as the lessons Saturn has to teach you. The following table briefly describes the lesson of Saturn in each sign.

Saturn Astro Sign	Saturn's Lesson
Saturn ♄ in Aries ♈	Learn independence and self-reliance.
Saturn ♄ in Taurus ♉	Learn to be less selfish; see that the material is not all-important.
Saturn ♄ in Cancer ♋	Learn to fulfill your own emotional needs and work with family.
Saturn ♄ in Leo ♌	Learn to unleash your creativity and inner child.
Saturn ♄ in Virgo ♍	Learn to let go of your drive and worries and enjoy the simple life.

173

Saturn Astro Sign	Saturn's Lesson
Saturn ♄ in Libra ♎	Learn to work and cooperate with others to strengthen your relationships.
Saturn ♄ in Scorpio ♏	Learn to use your power wisely and to discard doubt.
Saturn ♄ in Sagittarius ♐	Learn patience and perseverance and develop introspection.
Saturn ♄ in Capricorn ♑	Learn flexibility in dealing with others and learn to build on solid foundations.
Saturn ♄ in Aquarius ♒	Learn to free yourself of inhibition and excessive self-control and to create vision in a concrete way.
Saturn ♄ in Pisces ♓	Learn to trust in yourself and your intuition and to understand your own boundaries.

Now let's look at a birth chart and see where Saturn is, and what the lessons are. Look back to Jennifer Lopez's chart in Chapter 4. Jennifer has Saturn ♄ in Taurus ♉ in her 9th house. She's very determined and responsible, but must learn to be less self-involved, and less focused on material gain. Jennifer will need to learn not to let her material preoccupation take over in business with partners. She must learn the balance between partners when it comes to money or values. She also needs to know what is going on in her financial and business contracts—it's important for her not to delegate her financial responsibilities (or resources) to others.

Now take a look at your own birth chart and see what lesson Saturn ♄ is trying to teach you. Just knowing what the lesson is can be helpful in learning it—you may find that you've been struggling against this very issue for some time! Look at your family members' birth charts as well, and make notes about their Saturn lessons in your Intuitive Arts notebook. Saturn can provide you with more insight into your relationship; if your lesson is about flexibility in relationships, and your husband has to learn about patience, you may find that you both sometimes seem to come up short-tempered. Saturn is the planet that relates to doing your work and taking a serious approach to life's obstacles. Any obstacle or challenge that you find between family members should be welcomed as a learning experience, because that obstacle serves as a point of growth for the relationship. Saturn is the teacher and the taskmaster of the sky. Work on learning your Saturn lesson, and help your family members learn theirs—this will bring harmony to your family relationships.

Jupiter ♃: Growing with the Family

Jupiter ♃ symbolizes growth in your birth chart, and is also the planet of excess and overindulgence. Your possibilities for physical and intellectual development can be seen through Jupiter, as can your belief system. You won't see lessons in Jupiter, but you will see your potential for growth, as well as *how* you tend to grow through this planet. We've made notes on Jupiter ♃ in each sign here.

Jupiter ♃ in Aries ♈. You are independent and creative, and you grow through your enthusiasm. You are optimistic and look for the silver lining around every cloud!

Jupiter ♃ in Taurus ♉. You understand money, and you grow steadily. You find prosperity and enjoy the good things in life.

Jupiter ♃ in Gemini ♊. You are popular and intellectual, and you grow using your mental abilities. Exuberant and inquisitive, you like to share information for everyone's growth.

Jupiter ♃ in Cancer ♋. You are sympathetic and optimistic, and you grow through your emotions. You feel a natural kindness and concern toward others, and your family may include extended and created family!

Jupiter ♃ in Leo ♌. You are self-confident and charming, and you grow through generosity. You know that creating leadership and delegating to others develops esteem.

Jupiter ♃ in Virgo ♍. You are practical and methodical, and you grow through your pragmatism. You are devoted to a cause, and know that service to the community benefits the whole.

Jupiter ♃ in Libra ♎. You are cooperative and honorable, and you grow using your social skills. Adapting and facilitating groups is a skill of yours, and you're good at balancing relationships.

Jupiter ♃ in Scorpio ♏. You have great faith in yourself and a desire for truth, and you grow through your power. Intuitive and inquiring, you take that leap of faith others may not!

Jupiter ♃ in Sagittarius ♐. You are generous and optimistic, and you grow through your great passion. Adventurous and shooting for the stars, you follow your bliss!

Jupiter ♃ in Capricorn ♑. You are patient and have great integrity, and you grow through your accessibility. You persevere and are tenacious about your goals—you desire a win-win situation.

Jupiter ♃ in Aquarius ♒. You are tolerant and humanitarian, and you grow through your desire for change. You are unique and look to the future—you inspire others to envision.

Jupiter ♃ in Pisces ♓. You are creative and compassionate, and you grow through your imagination. Idealistic and hopeful, you will sacrifice for the good of the whole.

Look back again at Jennifer Lopez's birth chart in Chapter 4 to see how she grows with Jupiter ♃. Jennifer has Jupiter ♃ in Libra ♎ in her 2nd house. She is charming and cooperative (as well as morally conventional—that explains her marriages!), and she learns using her social skills—partnerships are very good for her personal growth. Jupiter in Libra is interested in keeping the peace among family and friends. Jennifer would want to be negotiator and peacemaker when it comes to family disputes. She places great value on traditions, the arts, beauty, and the aesthetics in life, and she would earn her income through the arts or beauty, or by creating her own enterprise. Jennifer would want to see her family cooperate and give and take with each other—she would understand the need to adapt to other people's needs. She is generous with her income and extends her generosity to the public or organizations that help others in need.

Where is Jupiter ♃ in *your* birth chart? Jupiter completes its orbit every 12 years, returning to the sign it was in when you were born. Each time it makes this transit, it brings with it great opportunities for your personal growth and development. You may have the opportunity to increase your earnings, get additional education, or find new aspirations during a Jupiter return. The wheel of life will feel like it has turned in your favor!

North Node ☊, South Node ☋: Karma Redux

The North Node ☊ and South Node ☋ also deal with issues of karma and karmic lessons. These are opposite each other on your birth chart and actually represent points in the Moon's orbit around the earth—they aren't planets. The South Node is representative of your past, or your past lives (your karma), and the North Node represents your future and your potential (your dharma). You may be more comfortable in the areas of your South Node—after all, this is what you know—but your greatest growth will be found in the area of your North Node, which is what you have to learn.

We believe that family members and those close to us are meant to help us learn our life lessons. So it would be helpful to know not only where your own Nodes are, but also those of close family members and friends—your parents, siblings, children, and best girlfriend may all be trying to help you reach your full potential, and you should be trying to help them. You can give yourself a head start by doing some birth chart research. We chose one of our sibling pairs from Chapter 2. Look back to that chapter for the charts of Venus Williams and Serena Williams.

Venus has her North Node ☊ in Leo ♌ in her 11th house, which places her South Node ☋ in Aquarius ♒ in her 5th house. She is using her skills in sports and self-expression, which are part of the realm of the 5th house, to expand her contributions to a global or universal level. Venus is learning to reach beyond herself to work for the common good of society, the humanitarian realm of the 11th house. She is also learning to use her talents and abilities to broaden her focus on life goals.

Serena has her North Node ☊ in nurturing Cancer ♋ in her 4th house of family; her South Node ☋ is in Capricorn ♑ in her 10th house of career. Her Libra ♎ Sun ☉ gives her a sense of balance and a desire for harmony, good support, and encouragement for her to move from her comfort base in career to the security and comfort of safe haven through family. Her bullish Taurus ♉ ascendant creates challenge for her, though, as it squares □ her North Node ☊. This is a challenge that she can rise to meet with the same intensity and determination she puts forth each time she steps onto the tennis court—and this challenge offers Serena tremendous opportunity for growth and learning on the karmic court as well.

The house placements of their North ☊ and South ☋ Nodes indicate the ways in which Venus and Serena will be able to help each other overcome fear of change. Serena can help Venus learn about 11th house (goals) or North Node issues because she has Mars ♂ in Leo ♌ conjunct Venus's North Node ♂ ☌ ☊. Venus, on the other hand, can help Serena learn about 4th house issues of family because her Mercury ☿ in Cancer ♋ is conjunct Serena's North Node ☿ ☌ ☊. These sisters have a lot to teach each other, and of course—as the concept of karmic lessons indicates—we are here to learn and grow and family is the place we start!

Where Are Your Nodes?

If you find that you have a fear of change, and that you have a difficult time breaking away from old and comfortable habits, that's the pull of your South Node ☋. Resist it! Whether you believe in past lives or not, the South Node ☋ relates to your past, and to what you know. While you need to use those skills in your life, and they can help you with the path of your North Node, they are also the areas it's most difficult for you to leave, and they can make it hard for you to break away and look to your North Node. It's the North Node ☊ that you should look toward if you want success in life and in family, and personal growth and development. It's not the easier path, but the fulfillment you get from following your North Node ☊ with be well worth the effort. The signs that the Nodes are in indicate elemental lessons to be learned; the house the Nodes fall in are the areas in which these lessons will surface in your life. Here are brief descriptions of the Nodes in each sign. Use these to help you interpret your own life lessons.

North Node ☊ in Aries ♈, South Node ☋ in Libra ♎. You know about harmony in relationships, and now have to learn how to express your individuality (while still maintaining that important balance).

North Node ☊ in Taurus ♉, South Node ☋ in Scorpio ♏. You know about power, spirituality, and transformation, and now must learn to establish roots, and discover what your values are and how to live by them.

North Node ☊ in Gemini ♊, South Node ☋ in Sagittarius ♐. You are understanding, and have a strong belief system. You must learn to express your beliefs—particularly in relationships—and to see past them to others' points of view.

North Node ☊ in Cancer ♋, South Node ☋ in Capricorn ♑. You know how to meet your career needs, and are practical and self-reliant. You must learn to give up some of your self-reliance, open up emotionally, and connect fully with others, especially your family.

North Node ☊ in Leo ♌, South Node ☋ in Aquarius ♒. You're tolerant and selfless—you believe in the greater good. You must learn to connect with individuals and think about what's best for each person on a one-to-one basis.

North Node ☊ in Virgo ♍, South Node ☋ in Pisces ♓. You're compassionate and sensitive, and you need to learn to apply those gifts to help people in practical ways.

North Node ☊ in Libra ♎, South Node ☋ in Aries ♈. You are a strong individual, and know how to express your individuality. You need to learn how to work with others, particularly in personal relationships, and recognize the equal importance of others in the world.

North Node ☊ in Scorpio ♏, South Node ☋ in Taurus ♉. You're very grounded and know how to build a solid foundation in life. You must learn to move beyond these foundations, accept change, and continue to grow.

North Node ☊ in Sagittarius ♐, South Node ☋ in Gemini ♊. You're curious and enjoy learning new things, and now must learn to take what you know and work on developing an understanding of the bigger picture.

North Node ☊ in Capricorn ♑, South Node ☋ in Cancer ♋. You are compassionate and supportive, and a good nurturer. You must learn self-reliance and work on personal responsibility.

North Node ☊ in Aquarius ♒, South Node ☋ in Leo ♌. You are very loving and generous, but also self-involved. You need to see the bigger picture, and learn to serve others.

North Node ☊ in Pisces ♓, South Node ☋ in Virgo ♍. You are analytical and have a great understanding of the physical plane of existence. You must learn to balance the physical with the spiritual, and develop your intuition and empathy.

What's in Your 12th House?

The 12th house in your birth chart is the house of the subconscious mind and past karma. It's a mystical house, and one that links your subconscious to reality. If you can figure out what you have going on in this house, you can learn those karmic lessons and move on to new ones. If you spend your whole life out of touch with this side of yourself—the intuitive, emotional side (this is the house of Pisces ♓)—well, you'll likely spend a lot of time repeating those life lessons, and you may be out of touch with yourself in a way that causes you to engage in self-destructive behaviors.

So let's look at someone's 12th house, and see what lessons this person has to learn to move beyond daily worries and into an awareness of the subconscious mind and a higher state of being. Turn back to Goldie Hawn's birth chart in Chapter 3. Goldie is a Scorpio ♏, a very intense Sun ☉ sign. She has Mercury ☿ and the asteroids Vesta ⚶ and Ceres ⚳ in her 12th house, all in Sagittarius ♐. Mercury ☿ in this house is very contemplative, and may require time to make decisions. You never know what Goldie is really thinking; her conscious mind is connected to her subconscious. She can absorb thoughts and ideas well. Vesta is the hearth and home and Ceres is the green thumb. Goldie's need to form a plan of action is necessary for her mind to remain calm. It's as though she incubates her feelings on the subject first and then will come forth with her plan of action. She may or may not be aware of this process, but it is her creativity at its best—like giving birth!

Now look at your own birth chart. What do you have in your 12th house? If there are no planets there, you need to look at the sign on your natal 12th house to find the planetary ruler for the house—the house is ruled by the planet that rules the sign in your 12th house. Confused? Arlene has Aquarius ♒ on her natal 12th house, so Arlene has Uranus ♅ ruling her 12th house. Cathy has Pisces ♓ on her natal 12th house, so Cathy has Neptune ♆ ruling her 12th house.

If you do have planets in this house, see what they are and consider what they might mean to you regarding your karma and your subconscious mind. Don't forget to note what signs they are in. You can look at family members' birth charts as well, and note what their influences are. If you know the karmic issues your family members are dealing with, you can help them through their lessons, and you can also use this information to understand why they behave as they do sometimes.

The Tarot Horseshoe Spread

The Tarot Horseshoe Spread uses five cards to look at how your past lives, or your karma, affects the lessons you are learning now.

Tarot's Horseshoe Spread.

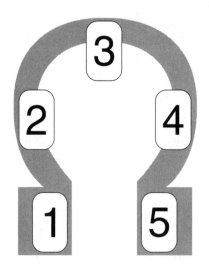

You can do this spread for yourself, or you can ask a question about you and a family member, and apply the reading to a family issue or concern. Arlene did the following reading for Chris, who wanted to know if he would be able to work out some difficulties he was having with his teenaged son, Jake. Chris's spread follows.

Chris's Horseshoe Spread: Will Chris work out his difficulties with his son Jake?

Queen of Pentacles. The first card in the spread deals with how your karma affects the question asked. This queen is productive and generous. This queen can represent Jake's mother or a woman who can help, and she looks as though she nurtures well and will give what she can to Jake. Chris needs to ask this queen for help getting over the hurdles he faces in his relationship with his son Jake.

2 of Swords. The second card relates to the past lessons of your question in this life. This blindfolded woman sits in a place of indecision and confusion. Chris has a difficult time understanding how to approach his son. The blindfold indicates that Chris cannot see through his present difficulties and he needs time to analyze his feelings before making any direct communication with his son. Chris should study the situation Jake is in before he makes any decision to discipline or restrict Jake.

King of Cups. The third card shows where you are right now in relation to your question. What a good card for this placement! This is the humanitarian and heart-centered Father figure. Chris can be this man or this might be a man with helpful advice offering compassion and understanding. Chris may seek help from this man, or this may be part of Chris that needs to come forward: the benevolent king who can put himself in the shoes of others, in order to understand them and identify problems early and easily.

The Emperor. The fourth card shows the lessons you are learning now, related to the question. The emperor is the authoritarian patriarch, and this card may indicate that Chris needs to work on this side of his personality and his relationship with Jake. Perhaps he needs to take a stronger leadership role in their relationship—Chris is learning what parenting is all about! The Emperor card asks Chris to use logic and reason with his son. Chris will need to be a strong Father without directing anger or angst toward his son. He should create an atmosphere of leadership and have wise sit-down-and-talk sessions with Jake. This may impress upon Jake Chris's sincere desire to come to a resolution.

5 of Pentacles R. The final card deals with your future karmic lessons related to your question. This card reversed indicates the development of compassion and the acceptance of loss. The lessons being learned between Father and Son will be able to heal. This card indicates the power to stop a negative cycle from getting worse, and the need for understanding two very different points of view and integrating them into a whole. Compromise on both sides will help the relationship heal. Chris and Jake should consider a contract or commitment of honoring each other's individuality. With such mutual respect, things can and will turn around. If they accept each other's faults, they might find optimism in what they learn from the experience.

Your Family Horseshoe Spread

Now try the Tarot Horseshoe Spread for yourself. Begin by thinking of a question you have for yourself or relating to a family relationship. Write the question down here, or make your notes on the reading in your Intuitive Arts notebook.

My Tarot Horseshoe Spread question:

_____

Now, think about the question while shuffling the Tarot deck. When you're ready, lay out the cards. Don't forget to record the reading in your Intuitive Arts notebook! This reading can be helpful to you with a family relationship, as it can help you to see sides of the issue—the karmic aspects—you might not otherwise be aware of.

Tarot's 10s: The House You're Building

What kind of house do you and your family live in? Do you have a dream house? What kind of house—or houses—did you grow up in? For this Psychic Intuition exercise, we'd like you to gather together some family photos of you at home at different ages, including where you live now. You can choose photos of the inside of your home or the outside, and other people can be in the photos or not. It doesn't matter whether your home is, or was, a townhouse, an apartment, a suburban rancher, a mobile home, a farmhouse, or something else altogether. Gather some photos, and while you're at it, gather photos of the homes your siblings and other family members live in now. Keep these photos separate from the others, and move on to the next step.

Let's take a look at Tarot's 10s as we work through this exercise. The number 10 is the number of completion and moving into a new beginning at the same time. The number 10 also indicates that family group has been working together for a long period of time. When we start with the Ace, we are working toward an area of life on our own. When the numbers get higher in the Tarot, we have put in more effort or added more people to the situation. How do humans learn? By relating to other humans. The family is a special grouping of people who are in it for the long haul. No getting around it, you have your family or the lessons of your family for life.

10 of Wands: Burdened by family responsibility and the desire to carry more than required, family issues and relationships are being strained. The 10 of Wands R can indicate that the family is releasing their burdens and is able to regain their energy as a group. Family members have the power to change their dynamics by not allowing for any form of manipulating power into the family.

Now that you have the photos, arrange them in some way—chronologically may be the easiest, though if you moved around a lot, you might prefer to arrange them geographically, and you could also choose to order your homes from favorite to least favorite. Do this step however you like. Once the photos are arranged, study each one carefully, noting in your Intuitive Arts notebook the physical details of the place, as well as your mental images and the emotional memories the photo recalls. How do you feel about the house, and what does the photo say to you? What were you like when you lived there, what was life like, and what was your family like? Did you live there alone or with family members? Were you happy or unhappy there, and why?

Now spread out the photos of the homes you and your family members live in now. What do they look like? How do they make you feel? Note the differences and similarities between them, and then look at each one, and compare it to the homes you had previously in your life. Note any similarities and differences. Which of your previous homes is your present home most like? Which is it most unlike? Look back at your notes on each place, to see whether the home you are making for yourself and your family now is like a place you recall fondly or one where you were unhappy. Do this for your family members as well.

Why do you think you've chosen the home you have now? Are you repeating a happy home from your childhood? A sad one? Are you breaking away from unhappy memories? What do you feel your home says about you today? While you likely had little or no control over where you lived as a child or what your home looked like, as an adult you have much more choice, and are creating your own home for yourself and your family. Are you creating the home you want?

10 of Pentacles: Stability and multigenerational prosperity, and traditional or cultural acceptance, reveal the family is able to remain secure and content. Stability of a lasting nature is indicated in this card upright. Financial security and community reputation is sound. The generations have successfully passed down prosperity and wisdom of the material world. 10 of Pentacles R indicates loss or uncertainty in the family or the family's wealth. A poor investment or insecurity may face the family now. Resources need to be kept in check, and the family needs to regroup, focusing on the basics and not the power to accumulate.

10 of Swords: The end of one lifestyle and completion of a karmic lesson places the goal of the 10 of Swords in family as the power to leave behind old patterns that have caused pain. The 10 of Swords R is crisis within family. The lesson of the 10 of Swords is to work with the crisis, be it divorce or severing of ties—all families have their ups and downs. Healing will come with the 10 of Swords R, for the crisis has passed and tomorrow is a new day.

Go back to that dream home. Close your eyes and imagine it. What kind of home is it, and how does it feel? How do you feel inside this home? Does your dream home represent a departure or repetition of some kind of the home you have now or one of the homes you lived in as a child? What is it you're trying to leave behind or repeat?

10 of Cups: Happily ever after. This is the card we all wish for. The 10 of Cups upright is the bliss and joy of the family working together in a continual process of love. All members of this family believe in the love of life and they love one another as individuals. This card represents children, home, and the emotional security of knowing you are welcomed in the family. When the 10 of Cups is reversed, there is a need to pay attention to the family and to not take any family member for granted. Someone may not be happy in the home or family when you get this card reversed—find out who, and why. This person needs emotional support and compassion.

This can be a useful and fun exercise to do with family members—the stroll down memory lane may be happy or sad, but it's sure to evoke lots of shared memories for everyone. Don't be surprised, however, if those memories aren't the same for everyone. A home you recall as happy may be remembered quite differently by a sibling. Try to figure out what you and your family members are trying to create for yourselves now in terms of a home, and why. How can you help one another achieve those dreams of family and home? This can help you maintain the bonds you share as a family.

chapter 9

Create Your Home Blueprint

Your true dream home
What about what you *need* in a family?
Tarot's Celtic Cross
An astrological chart for your family's special day
Clarify and center your home environment with Feng Shui

If you could create a blueprint for your dream home, what would it be? We try and help you figure that out in this chapter. Detailing the layout and contents of your perfect family life, your home blueprint will emerge to show your hopes and dreams, empathy and generosity, goals and desires on the Intuitive Arts path toward nurturing the home and family you love. We want you to think about your dream family, and we also use Astrology to help you discover what you need in your family. We show you Tarot's Celtic Cross Spread, and how it can help you make your dream family a reality. Then we show you how to use an astrological event chart to plan for a future family event. Finally, we explore the ancient Chinese art of Feng Shui, and show you how its basic ideas can help you use Psychic Intuition to create the harmonious home you need to welcome your dream family into.

Your True Dream Home

In the last chapter, we did an exercise in which we asked you to look at the physical homes you have lived in during your lifetime. Then we talked about your dream home, and what it would look and feel like. Now we want you to think about the family who would live inside that home. What would your dream family look like? We want you to think about this question, because we come back to it throughout this chapter, as we help you plan the family you want.

What About What You Need in a Family?

We've been talking a lot about what you want in a family, but we can't forget to look at what you *need*, as well. We begin to look for what we need by assembling our birth charts, and assessing our Elemental Family Signature. We first introduced this in Chapter 3. You need to look at your birth chart and find the astrological signs for the Sun ☉, Moon ☽, Mercury ☿, Venus ♀, and Mars ♂, as well as your rising sign, or ascendant. Remember that the personal planets indicate how we truly are to our loved ones and the close associates in our lives. The rising sign or ascendant represents how we *appear* to others in the community. We've done this exercise for ourselves, and charted the astrological signs and the Element for each of these planets and the ascendant. First, we found Arlene's Elemental Family Signature.

Arlene's Birth Chart

Planet	Sign	Element
Ascendant	Pisces ♓	Water
Sun ☉	Aquarius ♒	Air
Moon ☽	Gemini ♊	Air
Mercury ☿	Aquarius ♒	Air
Venus ♀	Capricorn ♑	Earth
Mars ♂	Scorpio ♏	Water

Next, we wrote down the Element for each of these signs and then used the following table to tally how many planets Arlene has in each Element.

Element	Number of Signs
Fire	0
Earth	1
Air	3
Water	2

Arlene's Elemental Family Signature is Air, though she also has a healthy dose of Water thrown in. Air is an intellectual Element, and this signature indicates the importance of thinking, communication, and social interaction for Arlene. With her Moon ☽ in Gemini ♊, Arlene is curious and talkative, and she tends to be analytical about her feelings. When it comes to family, Arlene needs intellectual stimulus from family members to feel connected to them. She needs a verbal response or ongoing banter to feel emotionally connected.

Now let's look at Cathy's Elemental Family Signature:

Cathy's Birth Chart

Planet	Sign	Element
Ascendant	Taurus ♉	Earth
Sun ☉	Pisces ♓	Water
Moon ☽	Pisces ♓	Water
Mercury ☿	Pisces ♓	Water
Venus ♀	Aries ♈	Fire
Mars ♂	Scorpio ♏	Water

Now to see how many signs Cathy has in each Element:

Element	Number of Signs
Fire	1
Earth	1
Air	0
Water	4

With four Water signs, Cathy's Elemental Family Signature is Water. She is emotional and intuitive, and also creative. She feels through her imagination, and tends to think the very best of people. Three of those four Water signs are Pisces ♓, making Cathy's link to this sign very strong. Cathy would need to feel *needed* and nurtured in her family. The Elemental Water signature needs to feel attached to the mission of the family. The Water sign Pisces ♓ is a sign of devotion and compassion, so she would need devotion and compassion from the members of her family, and would give it in kind. Sensitive and intuitive, she would respond well to thoughtfulness—and hugs would be welcome often!

And in the 4th House of Family ...

In our search for what we need in family, Arlene and Cathy looked at their 4th house of family to see what planets are working there, as well as at the 3rd and 5th houses. The 3rd house relates to knowledge and siblings, and the 5th house concerns creativity and children.

Arlene's 3rd, 4th, and 5th Houses

House	Planet(s)	Astro Sign(s)
3rd	Moon ☽	Gemini ♊
4th	Uranus ♅	Cancer ♋
5th	Lilith ⚸	Cancer ♋

In her 4th house of family, Arlene has Uranus ♅ in Cancer ♋; her 3rd house holds her Moon ☽ in Gemini ♊, and in her 5th house, we found Lilith ⚸, the asteroid, also in Cancer ♋. Lilith is called the Dark Moon, and represents the desire for freedom and independence from a traditional female role. Not all astrologers will use the asteroids in interpreting a chart, unless that is the only planet in a particular house. (Read more about Lilith ⚸ in Appendix A.) In Arlene's case, Lilith is the only planet in her 5th house. Uranus ♅ in her 4th house marks Arlene as independent, and perhaps quite different from the rest of her family. She may find her home life marked by sudden changes through her life. Uranus ♅ here also indicates that Arlene might use her home for meetings, which she does for her work on a regular basis. In regards to family, Arlene has always been allowed to say what she feels to her parents and siblings. Many a debate about any topic you might think of has been held at the Sunday dinner table in her house.

Arlene's independent nature started early in life. As her father said when she was 5 years old, Arlene always wanted her own way of doing things. Arlene says she was self-assertive about how her room appeared and what type of friends she would bring home. Unique and unconventional in her approach to family, Arlene brought home folks from all walks of life; this helped fulfill her desire for independence, free thinking, speaking her mind, and enjoying mental stimulus. This applies to her life today as well! Arlene has connected to all walks of life not only because of her work, but also because she needs the stimulus of new thought, new ideas, new values. The future is always on her mind and she progresses toward that end in her home. And she constantly relates her new discoveries and insights to her family for them to mull over!

From her family, Arlene needs freedom to express her needs and a nontraditional approach. Arlene did not get that in her early years, but as she grew and her parents trusted her judgment, Arlene has more acceptance from her parents. Uranus in the 4th house can make you suddenly move or change residence, and Arlene did move away from home to a new city and state where she had never been before nor knew anyone: Seattle, Washington. Arlene's 4th house Uranus ♅ in the Cardinal sign Cancer also makes her want to create an atmosphere of understanding and peace for all who enter her home.

Here are Cathy's planets in these houses:

Cathy's 3rd, 4th, and 5th Houses

House	Planet(s)	Astro Sign(s)
3rd	Mercury ☿ (ruling)	Gemini ♊
4th	Jupiter ♃, Juno ⚶	Cancer ♋, Leo ♌
5th	Pluto ♀	Virgo ♍

Cathy has no planets in her 3rd house of siblings, so we look at the natural ruler of the sign Cathy has on the 3rd house's cusp—Gemini ♊. In her 4th house of family, Cathy has Jupiter ♃ in Cancer ♋ as well as the asteroid Juno ⚶ in Leo ♌. In her 5th house, she has Pluto ♀ in Virgo ♍. With Jupiter ♃ in her 4th house, Cathy is comfortable at home, and probably had a happy childhood. She's warm and compassionate, and likely comes from a large family. ("All true!" she says.) Cathy has a need to nurture others and she can see potential in everyone. Cathy's Jupiter and Juno in her 4th house certainly draw her into creating her own family and home life to be secure, stable, and healthy for all she is responsible for. Home is her castle, and she will do better working from the home. Then she can have everything around her that she is attached to. Jupiter in the 4th house would indicate an expansive home or adding children. (Cathy says, "!!") And there is an increase in family fortune or prosperity. Cathy will become empowered by her relationships to her children and her children may in fact inspire change in her career or parenting skills. Cathy's children will help her evolve beyond the parameters she was taught as a child. Sometimes, her children will actually parent her!

Your Family Needs

Now take a look at your own birth chart, and use the following tables to track your Elemental Family Signature (or look back at your notes from Chapter 3), and to note the planets you have in your 3rd, 4th, and 5th houses.

191

Your Elemental Family Signature

Planet	Astro Sign	Element
Ascendant	_____	_____
Sun ☉	_____	_____
Moon ☽	_____	_____
Mercury ☿	_____	_____
Venus ♀	_____	_____
Mars ♂	_____	_____

Now see how many signs you have in each Element:

Element	Number of Signs
Fire	_____
Earth	_____
Air	_____
Water	_____

What's your Elemental Family Signature, and what does it say about you and what you need in family?

Now, fill in the planets and signs in your 3rd, 4th, and 5th houses.

Your 3rd, 4th, and 5th Houses

House	Planet(s)	Astro Sign(s)
3rd	_____	_____
4th	_____	_____
5th	_____	_____

What planets do you have in each of these houses? Can you look at these houses and see what the planets and signs mean in terms of your own family needs? Think about what the planets say about you, and what this, in turn, indicates about what will work best for you in family. Does what you *want* in family mesh with what you *need?* If so, great! Combine the two and start working on fulfilling your needs and your dreams! If the two don't mesh, you might want to spend some time first thinking about how they differ, and why you want the family you do—you can still work on creating your dream family; if it's not in synch with your true needs, however, you might find that, once your dream comes true, you aren't happy and fulfilled after all.

If you can work to mesh the two, or compromise on a family ideal that meets both your wishes *and* your needs, your chances for success and family happiness will be much greater. Compromise can be very difficult, but through compromise and adaptation amazing growth and enhanced family dynamics are possible. When your ideals and desires are met through your adaptation or through compromise, you will see the family you have always wanted!

Tarot's Celtic Cross

The Celtic Cross Spread is the storyteller of the Tarot. The 10 cards tell the story of your question and allow for the answer to gradually reveal itself to the querent. If you want to know how to get your dream family, or if you ever will, this spread can answer your question and give you insight into why the answer is what it is.

Card 1. This card represents the querent (the person asking the question). We think that this, and all the cards in the spread, should be chosen by the querent, as he or she contemplates their question.

Card 2. This card represents opposing forces, and can be supportive of the querent. This card is always placed upright in the spread. (Even if it turns up reversed, it will be turned upright for the reading.)

Card 3. This card looks at the foundation of the question—why did you ask it?

Card 4. This card is your past experience with the question. This has already happened, so it can't be changed, but it's also finished with.

Card 5. This is the energy around you right now. You can change this in the future. You can access this card by choosing to or you can avoid this card by your choice.

Card 6. This is what will happen in the future. The event that this card represents will reveal what needs to be accepted. You can't change this.

Card 7. This card represents your fears or your attitude about the question.

Card 8. This card represents how others feel about your question. Since we're talking about family, your family members likely are those represented by this card.

Card 9. This card shows your positive feelings about the question, and indicates what you need to do to get to the final card.

Card 10. This is the final outcome—the answer to your question!

Once you've read through these, take a look at the following Celtic Cross Spread. Arlene did this reading for Lydia, who asked if her dream family would ever be realized.

Lydia's Celtic Cross Spread: Will my dream family become a reality?

The Sun R. This is Lydia. She's on a rocky path right now, which may be related to some difficulty from her childhood. The Sun in its reversed position also represents the conditions around Lydia, who may be pessimistic about her dream family becoming a reality because of childhood issues or because her more recent experiences have not resulted in the dream she anticipated.

5 of Wands. The opposing forces. This card indicates struggle—isn't that what the card looks like? There isn't any focus with this card, and the energy is scattered. Lydia is anxious about the conditions around her now and there might have been opposition or nonsupportive energy from others who might have asked, "Do you really think the dream family exists?" She needs to stand her ground and be strong through any opposition to her goal.

Ace of Cups. Why is Lydia asking the question? This card represents the opening of the heart. Lydia may be asking this question now because she is more open and now truly wants this family life. Lydia has a good perspective on her life; she wants love and joy and desires the contentment of a dream family. She has the right attitude toward her desired goal, which is love.

Page of Swords. Lydia's past experiences regarding her question. This card may indicate delay or disappointment related to the question, meaning that Lydia's experience with her dream family has not been successful in the past. Possibly she had some difficulty in her childhood that she is remembering and dealing with now. The Page of Swords reminds Lydia of that past. It's the messenger of caution and remembering—Lydia remembers the sorrows or upsets of the past, but she must also remind herself that this position in the Celtic Spread is the *past*—she can't change it now, but she can move beyond it.

King of Cups. The energy around Lydia now. This is a compassionate, humanitarian card. Lydia has some very positive family energy around her now! A supportive, emotional, and sensitive king may be coming into Lydia's life! She may already be around him at this time. The King of Cups is a man of devotion and loyalty, and a good Father figure. He can bring the dream family into reality with Lydia. A man of the heart, this king will support Lydia's ideals and goals.

9 of Pentacles R. What's in the future for Lydia that she cannot change? This card reversed indicates that Lydia will be dissatisfied with her home environment in the future. She might feel a loss of security. What event could this reversed 9 of Pentacles relate to? Lydia might not be able to get the financial goal of the dream family together as quickly as she wants. Financial success takes time—sometimes years—to create in family. This card would tell Lydia to reflect upon the idea that she needs to work on the reality of money management and not just the dream of creating it.

Queen of Swords R. Lydia's fears related to her question. Reversed, this card indicates loss and a tendency toward being judgmental. Lydia may fear that in trying to create her dream family, she may experience the loss of her family or of some family members. Lydia may also fear another woman will intervene or influence her dream family when it finally arrives in her life. Influence on a negative level shows in this card, but remember, these are Lydia's fears and not necessarily what will happen. Lydia may need to meditate on that fear to release it from her own psyche. She may worry about whether her dream family will last when she finally has it. The Queen of Swords R can represent a facet of Lydia's personality or a fear of other influences ruining her dream family.

9 of Wands R. How Lydia's family feels about the question. This card indicates physical and mental exhaustion, and possibly worry. Lydia's family may feel the need for some thinking and regrouping time before embarking on any major changes. Her family will want a strong relationship for her when she creates her own family, but they are also anxious for her. They may be worried that she could fail to meet her ultimate goal. Her family knows how sensitive Lydia is and is likely aware of the struggles she has had in her life. They are very protective of her and worry about her high ideals leading to disappointment.

Page of Pentacles R. The positive feelings around the question. This card indicates delays and a lack of motivation—it doesn't sound too positive, does it? Remember that this is also what Lydia must work through to get to the answer in the final card. Pages can represent children. Lydia may have to decided about the role of children in her life—if and when to have them, will there be enough financial support for them? Pentacles represent resources, so we would surmise that Lydia will get to work on her financial outlook before deciding to add new members to her dream family.

Judgement R. The final outcome. This card reversed indicates a fear that happiness won't be found, and can also indicate a delay. Lydia's final card is a Major Arcana card. Lydia's dream family will be realized, but she first needs to understand that everything she wants will take time—her goal may be realized one stepping-stone at a time. She may want it all to happen at once, but Judgment R means she needs to be realistic about how long it will take. Her dream family may be a work in progress over a number of years. Judgement R indicates that Lydia should take her goal one day at a time and perhaps even one smaller goal at a time. She should build upon what she has and can do rather than hope for what might happen. Lydia's goals are attainable with time, effort, and supportive people. She may change some of her original goals as she develops her dream family. What she wanted at the beginning in her vision may not be what she stays with—she may wisely readjust her original thoughts into new goals. Time is on her side.

This is how the cards worked out for Lydia. You should now try the Celtic Cross Spread for yourself, and ask yourself any family question—perhaps you'll want to start by asking the same question as Lydia: *Will my family dream come true?* For this question to be answered, you must have given some thought to that family dream, and have a pretty clear idea what you want in your dream family. Use the following blank Celtic Cross Spread as a reminder of where to place your cards.

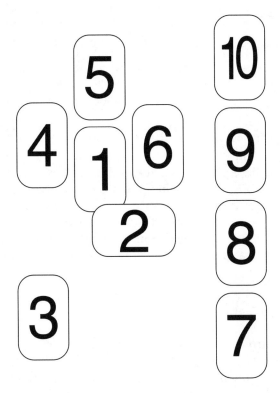

Your Celtic Cross Tarot spread.

Begin by shuffling the Tarot deck while thinking of your question. Then lay out the cards in order, from 1 to 10. Use Lydia's reading for help if you need it. Record your cards and your impression of each card here or in your Intuitive Arts notebook.

Card 1: _____ This card is you.

Card 2: _____ Opposing forces.

Card 3: _____ Why are you asking this question?

Card 4: _____ Your past experiences concerning your question.

Card 5: _____ The energy around you now.

Card 6: _____ The future, that which you cannot change.

Card 7: _____ Your fears about the question.

Card 8: _____ How your family feels about your question.

Card 9: _____ Positive feelings around the question.

Card 10: _____ The answer to your question!

What answer did you find for your question? If the answer isn't clear to you, perhaps your question wasn't clear (or you aren't really sure what you're asking). Remember that only the fourth and sixth cards represent destined elements of the question; everything else is up to you! Perhaps you need to spend some time working on your fears, or talking to your family members about what they want in a dream family, before you can expect your dream to become a reality.

An Astrological Chart for Your Family's Special Day

You can use Astrology to help plan for a future event—or to look back at a past event and see why it didn't go as planned. Look ahead to a planned family reunion or a wedding and see what kind of day it will be for you, and for family members. To do this, you need to create an event chart; an astrologer can do this for you.

Event Charts and Progressions

An event chart is a chart created for a particular date, in the past or the future. As you move through your life, and experience its ups and downs, the planets progress, as well. An astrologer can create an event chart that will show the planets at any particular time. You might want to see a chart for one of those occasions previously mentioned, or for a day in the past—perhaps your Pluto ♇ transit. We looked at this in Chapter 6, and included a Pluto transit chart for Goldie Hawn. If you recall that chart, it included Goldie's birth chart on the inside of the astrological wheel, and her Pluto transit chart on the outside—it's called a bi-wheel chart, and it shows you where the planets were at your birth (natal), and where they have moved to from that day to the day of your planned event (transit chart). (A progressed chart, on the other hand, essentially moves the planets one day for each year from your birth. Progressed charts are based only on your natal chart—the planetary movement is symbolic—and they deal with your internal and psychological growth.) To better explain the use of event charts, we've created one for Ozzy Osbourne to the date of the premiere of his MTV television show, *The Osbournes*.

The inner wheel of this bi-wheel chart is Ozzy's solar birth chart; the outer wheel is a chart for the day of his television show premiere on MTV—March 5, 2002. On the day of the show's New York premiere, the Moon ☽ was in Sagittarius ♐, which is Ozzy's Sun ☉ sign. It is an amazing find in Astrology when a birth chart is aspected by transits that support what is happening! The idea of comparing charts allows you to see the powerful energy in the sky, and how it enhances the potential in a birth chart. Ozzy's premiere certainly connects back to his original solar chart. Ozzy is a Sagittarius ♐, and the transiting Moon on that day was over his natal Sun! That same transiting Moon in Sagittarius is conjunct the transiting Pluto in Sagittarius ☽ ☌ ♇. Sagittarius deals with promotion and the Moon deals with the public, so this was a perfect day for the premiere. Pluto, representing the collective public, conjunction is transiting in Ozzy's solar 10th house of career and public recognition. The show would bring Ozzy much attention and publicity, just as he received at the height of his rock-and-roll career.

Transiting Jupiter ♃ in Cancer ♋ opposes his natal Jupiter ♃ in Capricorn ♑ and natal Mars ♂ in Capricorn ♑. Jupiter ♃ is Ozzy's natal Sun ☉ ruler, so this event brings the public into his personal life. The public will get to see the Osbourne home, the family, and how the family relates! The show may not last long, but the exposure allows us to see that everyone has a family and real family lessons to be learned. Transiting Mars in Taurus ♉ conjuncts Ozzy's natal North Node in Taurus ♂ ☌ ☊ and the transiting ascendant is conjunct Ozzy's natal South Node ☋ in Scorpio ♏. The public gets to see the crazy, obscure side of the family through the South Node ☋—they will see that Ozzy actually does have a family life and how he has gone up and down in his career. The prosperity of Taurus ♉ is also shown to us through the North Node ☊. The Osbournes truly have exposed themselves to us!

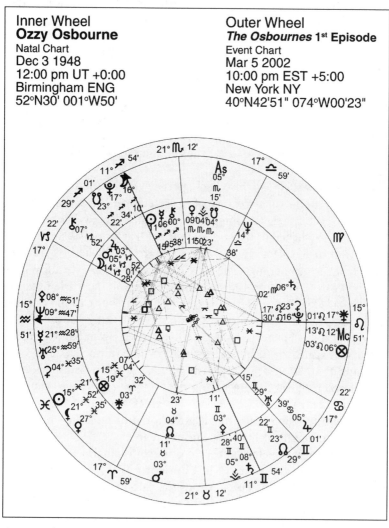

Inner Wheel
Ozzy Osbourne
Natal Chart
Dec 3 1948
12:00 pm UT +0:00
Birmingham ENG
52°N30' 001°W50'

Outer Wheel
***The Osbournes* 1ˢᵗ Episode**
Event Chart
Mar 5 2002
10:00 pm EST +5:00
New York NY
40°N42'51" 074°W00'23"

Ozzy Osbourne's event chart: the premiere of The Osbournes.

Using Event Charts and Tarot to Help with Future Family Plans

You can look ahead to a date you have for settling on your new home, or to the next big family holiday (Grandma's birthday, or Thanksgiving dinner), and use the information in your event chart to prepare yourself mentally for the day ahead. You can also do a Tarot reading for yourself with a question about that day, and draw cards on the day of the event to assess your own energy. Use astrological event charts for family members to help you understand what the day will be like for them, and if it looks like they won't be at their best, how to help them through it. If you have a date chosen for that family reunion, but from the event charts it looks like it will be a difficult time for you and close family members, you might want to choose a different date—and remember to look at the cycles of the Moon ☽ when planning events. The New Moon is the best time to begin new projects. It might not be within your power to change your son's wedding date, but you can use event charts to assess the energy for the day, and use your awareness to make things flow as smoothly as possible.

Clarify and Center Your Home Environment with Feng Shui

Feng Shui is an ancient art begun in China that posits that our lives and our destinies intertwine with nature and the world, and that all of this exists, in some form, within each of us, in our *chi*—our spirit or energy. There is also *chi* in the atmosphere and *chi* that moves within the Earth. It is the goal of Feng Shui to bring these energies—those within us and those that surround us—into alignment, and particularly to use the *chi* in our environment to make the *chi* in our bodies work better for us. Another way of looking at this is to try and balance our physical environments (our homes, our offices) with the natural world to make our spirits happier and more at peace.

Feng Shui is a fairly complicated art; there are various schools of Feng Shui and degreed practitioners out there whom you can hire to come in and adjust your home environment. They'll look at the positioning of everything in your home, including doorways, stairs, and windows, as well as the environment outside the house, the overall shape of the home, and its placement in relation to the Sun (north, south, east, west), which affects light and *chi*. Needless to say, we aren't going into all of that here—we aren't Feng Shui practitioners—but we do believe there are some simple ideas in Feng Shui that can be very useful in tapping into your Psychic Intuition to create a home environment that in turn lets you manifest the life—and family—you want.

What we're going to look at is *yi*, which is a way of using your own intuition to adjust the *chi*—the spirit—of your home. One component of *yi* is the eight areas of the *bagua*. Does this all sound a bit confusing? Stick with us a bit longer, and we'll make it worth your while! You'll recall from Chapter 2 that most energy can be thought of as *yin* or *yang*. *Yin* is the receptive, the indirect, the internal—the pull of the push/pull in family dynamics. *Yang* is the active, the direct, the external—the push of the push/pull in family dynamics. Somewhat like Astrology's wheel of houses, Feng Shui's bagua portrays the 8 *guas*, or areas of life: career and life work; knowledge, learning, and wisdom; family and health; abundance and prosperity; reputation and fame; love, marriage, and partnership; fertility, creativity, and children; and travel, generosity, and support. We've included a *bagua* here.

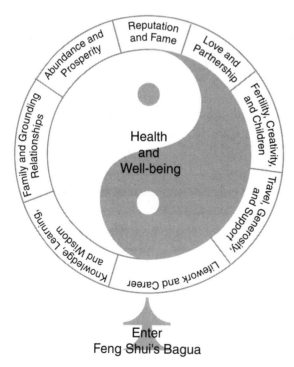

Feng Shui's bagua.

Feng Shui experts apply the *bagua* to an entire home and to rooms of the house. So if you're having difficulty with your family, or you just want to improve this area of your life, you should adjust this area of your home by moving furniture around (to open up blocked energy), or by applying one of the nine cures to the area to create harmony. The nine cures are light-refracting objects (mirrors, lights), sounds (wind chimes, bells), living objects (plants, a fish bowl), moving objects (a mobile, a fountain), heavy objects (rocks, statuary), electric appliances (TV, microwave, computer), bamboo flutes, colors, or other objects. Each of these cures is thought to alter in some way or to deflect the energy of the space.

We aren't going to be that specific here, and we want you to use your intuition in your own home environment. Do use the *bagua,* however, to get a feel for where each of these areas is in your home and within each room. Note that the *bagua* has directional indications. This is how you tell where the areas are in your home: Imagine the octagon overlaid on a room of your house with you standing in the doorway to enter it. Perhaps the area of family winds up along the far wall of your living room, or the area for children is behind the sofa! You might want to move the sofa to open up that flow of energy. Because you might not be able to change the structure of the house itself, or its placement (or at least not without extensive renovations!), you won't be able to move the family area from that wall, but what you can do is change the energy of that area—put a plant there, or hang a mirror in the area to visually open it up.

Because creating a harmonious and welcoming space for the family you want is our goal here, we'd like you to go through each room of your house, noting dark rooms and areas where the flow of movement feels blocked. You can use the *bagua* diagram (often portrayed as an octagon), but it might be just as helpful to first wander through your home with your Intuitive Arts notebook, making notes about the energy you feel in each room, and how easily you navigate the space. Do you have any plants? Is your home filled with light? Can you move easily from room to room without bumping into furniture? After making general notes, look at the *bagua* and see where the family area of each room is, and what that area looks and feels like.

After you've made these notes about your home, imagine yourself relaxed and peaceful in your dream home, where you and family live a happy and loving life. What does it feel like? What is the temperature? What kind of light and color do you see around you? The feeling of this place is the feeling of your spirit being happy and in harmony—this is what you need to create in your home! You can tell, intuitively, what you need to feel comfortable and secure (how did that dream home feel?) and these are likely the things you need in your home to make it feel like a harmonious place to be. Having your home reflect the life you want doesn't mean redecorating, buying new furniture, or hiring an interior designer; it has mainly to with how you feel, and very simple changes can alter how you feel. Once you feel secure and peaceful in your own home, you'll be able to approach your family life from another place—a place of harmony. And perhaps your family will feel the effects not only of that new plant in the corner, but also of your changed attitude.

Figuring out what your dream family looks like, and making your home a welcoming place for that family, is one step on your path toward fulfilling your family dream. We hope you'll use the other exercises in this book—and your newfound knowledge of Astrology, Tarot, and Psychic Intuition—to help you find your way. We're sure you can have the family you truly want, and we hope this book has brought you closer to an understanding of your family relationships and how to make them more harmonious. Now go and manifest the family of your dreams!

appendix A

Family Stars

The Wheel of the Zodiac
Planets in houses
Signs in houses
Planet personalities and rulers
House keywords
Elements, energies, and qualities
Aspects
It's all about family
Ordering birth charts and synastry grids online

This appendix contains a summary of Astrology's keywords and meanings to help you explore your family relationships through the signs, planets, and houses, and to interpret astrological birth charts. We also summarize the book's content, chapter by chapter, so you can go quickly to the information you want to know.

The Wheel of the Zodiac

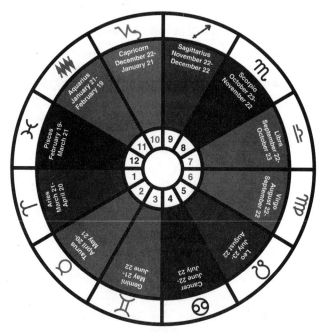

By the Signs

Here's a quick, handy reference to the astrological signs.

Aries, the Ram ♈   March 21 to April 20

Element	Fire
Quality	Cardinal
Energy	*Yang*
Rulers	Mars and Pluto
Anatomy	Brain, eyes, face
Keywords	Pioneering, initiating, beginnings

Taurus, the Bull ♉   April 20 to May 21

Element	Earth
Quality	Fixed
Energy	*Yin*
Ruler	Venus
Anatomy	Neck, throat, thyroid
Keywords	Ownership, dependability, sensuality

Gemini, the Twins ♊ May 21 to June 22

Element	Air
Quality	Mutable
Energy	*Yang*
Ruler	Mercury
Anatomy	Hands, arms, shoulders, lungs
Keywords	Mentality, communication, versatility

Cancer, the Crab ♋ June 22 to July 23

Element	Water
Quality	Cardinal
Energy	*Yin*
Ruler	Moon
Anatomy	Stomach, breasts
Keywords	Feeling, sensitivity, nurturing

Leo, the Lion ♌ July 23 to August 22

Element	Fire
Quality	Fixed
Energy	*Yang*
Ruler	Sun
Anatomy	Back, spine, heart
Keywords	Willpower, creativity, expressing the heart

Virgo, the Virgin ♍ August 22 to September 22

Element	Earth
Quality	Mutable
Energy	*Yin*
Ruler	Mercury
Anatomy	Intestines, colon
Keywords	Service, self-improvement, sacred patterns

Libra, the Scales ♎ September 22 to October 23

Element	Air
Quality	Cardinal
Energy	*Yang*
Ruler	Venus
Anatomy	Kidneys, lower back, adrenal glands
Keywords	Balance, harmony, justice

Scorpio, the Scorpion ♏ October 23 to November 22

Element	Water
Quality	Fixed
Energy	*Yin*
Rulers	Pluto and Mars
Anatomy	Genitals, urinary and reproductive systems
Keywords	Desire, transformation, power

Sagittarius, the Archer ♐ November 22 to December 22

Element	Fire
Quality	Mutable
Energy	*Yang*
Ruler	Jupiter
Anatomy	Liver, hips, thighs
Keywords	Understanding, enthusiasm, exploration

Capricorn, the Goat ♑ December 22 to January 21

Element	Earth
Quality	Cardinal
Energy	*Yin*
Ruler	Saturn
Anatomy	Bones, joints, knees, teeth
Keywords	Achievement, structure, organization

Aquarius, the Water Bearer ♒ January 21 to February 19

Element	Air
Quality	Fixed
Energy	*Yang*
Rulers	Uranus and Saturn
Anatomy	Ankles, circulation
Keywords	Humanitarian, unique, innovative

Pisces, the Fishes ♓ February 19 to March 21

Element	Water
Quality	Mutable
Energy	*Yin*

Pisces, the Fishes ♓   **February 19 to March 21**

Rulers	Neptune and Jupiter
Anatomy	Feet, immune system, hormonal system
Keywords	Compassion, universality, inclusiveness

By the Planets

Here's a quick, handy reference to the energy of each planet.

Planet	Symbol	Energies	Action Keyword
Sun	☉	Self, essence, life spirit, creativity, willpower	Explores
Moon	☽	Emotions, instincts, unconscious, past memories	Senses
Mercury	☿	Mental activities, communication, intelligence	Communicates
Venus	♀	Love, art, beauty, social graces, harmony, money, resources, possessions	Enjoys
Mars	♂	Physical energy, boldness, warrior ways, action, desires, anger, courage, ego	Acts
Jupiter	♃	Luck, abundance, wisdom, higher education, philosophy or beliefs, exploration, growth	Benefits
Saturn	♄	Responsibilities, self-discipline, perseverance, limitations, structures	Works
Uranus	♅	Sudden or unexpected change, originality, liberation, radical thinking authenticity	Innovates
Neptune	♆	Idealism, subconscious, spirituality, intuition, clairvoyance	Dreams
Pluto	♇	Power, regeneration, destruction, rebirth, transformation	Transforms

Signs in Houses

House	Astro Sign
1st	Aries ♈
2nd	Taurus ♉
3rd	Gemini ♊
4th	Cancer ♋
5th	Leo ♌
6th	Virgo ♍
7th	Libra ♎
8th	Scorpio ♏
9th	Sagittarius ♐
10th	Capricorn ♑
11th	Aquarius ♒
12th	Pisces ♓

Planetary Rulers

Planet	Signs Ruled
Sun ☉	Leo ♌
Moon ☽	Cancer ♋
Mercury ☿	Gemini ♊, Virgo ♍
Venus ♀	Taurus ♉, Libra ♎
Mars ♂	Aries ♈, co-ruler of Scorpio ♏
Jupiter ♃	Sagittarius ♐, co-ruler of Pisces ♓
Saturn ♄	Capricorn ♑, co-ruler of Aquarius ♒
Uranus ♅	Aquarius ♒
Neptune ♆	Pisces ♓
Pluto ♇	Scorpio ♏, co-ruler of Aries ♈

House Keywords

House	Key Term
1st	Identity
2nd	Self-worth
3rd	Knowledge
4th	Home and family
5th	Creativity
6th	Work and service

House	Key Term
7th	Relationships
8th	Transformation
9th	Beliefs
10th	Ethics and career
11th	Community
12th	Spirituality

Natural Planets and Natural Signs in Their Houses

Here are the natural planets and natural signs in their astrological houses.

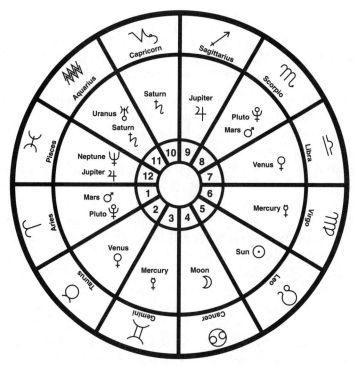

Asteroids and Planetoids

More than just the planets move through your birth chart! Here are the asteroids and the planetoid Chiron, and their areas of influence.

Asteroid	Realm	Areas of Influence
Ceres ⚳	Motherhood	Natural cycles, fertility, crops, relationships between parents and children
Juno ⚵	Marriage	Partnerships, contracts and agreements, social obligations
Pallas Athene ⚴	Wisdom	Intelligence, knowledge, understanding, equality
Vesta ⚶	Power	Sexuality, devotion, health, service to others
Planetoid		
Chiron ⚷	Healing	Transformation, personal growth

Aspects

Aspects are the geometric relationships between any two planets in your own chart, as well as in relation to another chart, whether for another person, a moment in time, or your own progressed chart. The main aspects to consider are as follows:

- **Conjunction** ☌   The strongest aspects. In a conjunction, the planets are placed at the same point on a chart or charts. Conjunctions are considered a focal point, with the interaction of the two planets emphasized.

- **Sextile** ⚹   In a sextile, the planets are 60° apart. The signs in a sextile share the same energy (*yin* or *yang*), so this is considered to be a favorable aspect.

- **Square** □   In a square, the planets are 90° apart. While squares are considered to be chart challenges, they often provide the impetus for change and improvement.

- **Trine** △   In a trine, the planets are 120° apart. This most favorable of the aspects means the planets share both element and energy. Trines indicate positive connections, often made so easily you may not even notice.

- **Opposition** ☍   In an opposition, the planets are 180° apart. There's little in common with an opposition, but, like squares, their difficult energy can spur us on to meet challenges.

- **Quincunx** ⚻   In a quincunx, the planets are 150° apart. Quincunxes are interesting—nothing is shared between the two signs, so some adjustment is usually required in order for them to interact.

Astrological Extras

The astrological charts and grids you see as examples throughout this book contain two symbols we don't include in our discussions (except for Arlene's chart in Chapter 8), but that might interest you in your further explorations of Astrology. These are the Part of Fortune ⊗ and the minor asteroid Lilith ⚸ . The Part of Fortune, sometimes called the Lot of Fortune, derives from ancient Astrology and represents the intersection in the Zodiac where your Sun ☉, Moon ☽, and ascendant converge. The Part of Fortune in its basic symbolism is a "point of karmic reward" in your birth chart. The ancients believed the Part of Fortune is what you would receive as a cosmic gift as you grew in this lifetime. Lilith, also called the Dark Moon, represents primal and emotional connections to your shadow side, and "liberation from conformity" in present-day interpretations.

It's All About Family

There are references to family and family issues all over your birth chart, but there are also some specific places to look for information on family. We've included Mel Gibson's birth chart, and have numbered some areas that deserve special attention when it comes to family.

1. In Chapter 1, we showed you where to look for your Sun ☉, which is your self, creativity, and will.

2. Also in Chapter 1, we introduced you to the houses in your birth chart; remember that the 4th house is the house of home and family.

3. In Chapter 2, you learned about your *yin/yang* equation: which planets have a *yin* quality and which have a *yang* quality, and how the energy of your chart can be compared with a family member's chart to find complementarity and balance in the relationship.

4. We also considered polarities between Sun signs in Chapter 2, and discussed the phases of the Moon ☽ in relation to family dynamics.

5. In Chapter 3, we introduced you to your Elemental Family Signature: how many personal planets you have in Fire, Earth, Air, and Water signs.

6. In Chapter 4, you learned how to identify the aspects in your 4th house, and how to read an aspect grid.

7. In Chapter 5, we introduced you to synastry, the astrology of relationships, and saw how your aspects (and your family members') can indicate compatibility.

8. Also in Chapter 5, we considered aspects created by the North ☊ and South ☋ Nodes, Saturn ♄, and Mars ♂, as well as retrograde ℞ planets, and how these aspects can be used to determine relationship longevity.

9. In Chapter 6, we took you for a stroll through the Moon ☽ signs to discover your emotional nature. You also learned where to look for your descendant and your nadir, to see how you connect with others and work within your family.

10. Also in Chapter 6, we looked at Saturn ♄ returns and Pluto ♀ transits, which can help you with individual and family growth.

11. In Chapter 7, you met the asteroids, Ceres ⚳, Juno ⚵, Pallas Athene ⚴, and Vesta ⚶, and saw what they can reveal about how you mother, partner, find strength, and commit. We also introduced you to Chiron ⚷, the wounded healer, and showed you how your psychic wound can be healed by those close to you—and how you help heal their wounds.

12. Also in Chapter 7, we explored the aspects in greater depth, including the conjunction ☌, sextile ⚹, square □, trine △, opposition ☍, and quincunx ⚻. We looked at how these supportive and challenging aspects influence relationships—and how they can help you move on if you must sever a family tie.

13. In Chapter 8, we looked at the lessons and growth your natal Saturn ♄ and Jupiter ♃ have in store for you.

14. Also in Chapter 8, you learned about karmic lessons and what the position of the Nodes ☋ ☊ on your birth chart can teach you about these. You also found the planets in your 12th house, and saw that you can learn your karmic lessons and move on—and help your family members to do so.

15. Finally, in Chapter 9, we showed you how to use your Elemental Family Signature and the 3rd, 4th, and 5th houses of your birth chart to determine what you *need* in family. Then we looked at event charts, and how they can help you prepare for a special family day.

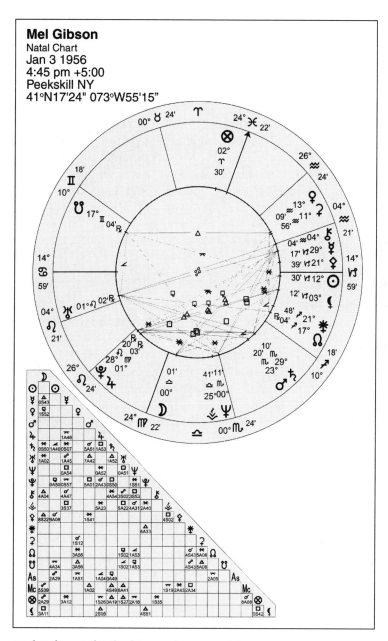

Mel Gibson's birth chart and aspect grid.

Ordering Birth Charts and Synastry Grids Online

Several websites will do birth charts for you. To get a birth chart that you can use with this book, be sure to specify that you want geocentric, Tropical Zodiac, Placidus house system, and True Node. Check out Arlene's site at www.mellinetti.com. Also check out Astrolabe, Inc., at www.alabe.com. This is the company that publishes Solar Fire, the computer software program Arlene used to generate the birth charts we used as examples throughout this book. A few other good Astrology websites include www.astro.com, www.astrodatabank.com, and www.stariq.com. But there are many astrological sites on the Internet; explore and choose the site that resonates to you and your investigation of Astrology, the heavens, and your family's place in the universe.

Birth Time and Your Birth Chart

The position of the Sun ☉ in the heavens at the time of your birth determines the placement of the planets and signs in the houses of your astrological birth chart. To know the precise position of the Sun, you need to know the location, date, and time of your birth. Many people don't know their birth times. There are various methods astrologers can use to cast birth charts when this is the case.

For the birth charts with unknown birth times that we used in this book, Arlene used the method called "noon chart." A noon chart uses noon as your time of birth, placing your Sun ☉ at the apex of the horoscope wheel—on your midheaven. Symbolically, this puts your soul at its highest potential in this lifetime, looking down with an eagle's-eye view, so to speak, on the planets and how they "fall" into place in the astrological houses to represent your life. Although there are some imprecisions with this or any method of casting a birth chart without a precise time of birth (for example, the ascendant sign changes every two hours), Arlene finds the noon chart allows the most accurate interpretations for the broadest range of people.

appendix B

Family Cards

No Tarot card's meaning is absolute, and for that reason, we encourage you to make personal interpretations of the cards, both by studying their individual images and examining the stories told by the cards' interrelationships. The images you see here are from the Universal Waite Tarot Deck published by U.S. Games Systems, Inc.

At the same time, knowing the traditional meanings of the cards can often give you an additional spin you might not have considered in your initial interpretation. That's why we've taken a fresh look at the cards' meanings as they apply specifically to family.

Tarot's Major Arcana

The Fool
New beginnings
Endless possibilities, optimism
Innocence and childhood

The Fool R
Uncertainty
A wrong direction
Look before you leap!

*The Magician
The power to
create our reality
Ask and ye shall
receive
A creative or
inventive person*

*The Magician R
Possibility of
manipulation
Lack of follow-
through
Inadequate use
of talent*

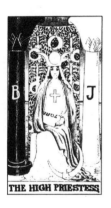

*The High Priestess
Intuition and
inner knowing
Yin and yang—
emotions + logic
Going with
your gut*

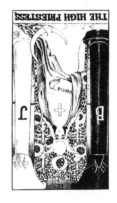

*The High Priestess R
Dream or illusion
A hidden agenda
Inaccurate
information*

*The Empress
A happy home
Fertility and
nurturance
An environment
for growth and
prosperity*

*The Empress R
Disagreements
at home
Family loss
Lack of security
or resources*

*The Emperor
Father figure
Past experience
can guide the
present
Ability to lead*

*The Emperor R
Insecurity and
immaturity
Stubbornness
Lack of leader-
ship*

*The Hierophant
Need for social
approval
Cultural
conformity
A solid spiritual
foundation*

*The Hierophant R
Nonconformist
behavior
Nontraditional
practices
Unorthodox ideas*

*The Lovers
New direction
for the heart
Good start for
a relationship
Desire for family
harmony*

*The Lovers R
Obstacles or
division
Delays
Indecision or
poor choices*

*The Chariot
Ability to meet
challenges
Focus and deter-
mination to
achieve goal
Positive outcome
after difficult time*

*The Chariot R
Confusion
Someone else
in control
A battle not
worth fighting?*

*Strength
The inner strength
of unconditional
love
Love without fear
The power of gen-
tle persuasion*

*Strength R
A power struggle
Intense emotions
that can lead
to upset
Feeling out of
control*

*The Hermit
Introspection
and solitude
A desire for truth
Trust own inner
voice for guid-
ance*

*The Hermit R
Inability to see
clearly
Wishing instead
of acting
Disregarding past
lessons*

The Wheel of Fortune Destiny comes calling! New family situation Change for the better

The Wheel of Fortune R Stagnation and indecision Missed opportunity Need to slow down and relax

Justice Fairness and a desire for balance A legal agreement or marriage Universal laws will prevail

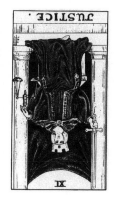

Justice R Unwise counsel Conditions that are out of balance Too much subjectivity

The Hanged Man Spiritual growth and enlightenment Need to reflect on the past Desire for a different lifestyle

The Hanged Man R Resistance to spiritual lessons Holding on to the past Fear of change

Death
Renewal and
transformation
A catalyst for
change
End of a cycle

Death R
Past blockages
impede progress
Stagnation and
stalemate
Arguments; too
tired to continue

Temperance
Good people
skills
Self-control,
balance, and
harmony
Patience and
perseverance

Temperance R
Impatience or
intolerance
Lack of good
judgment
Pushiness instead
of patience

The Devil
Obsession or
possessiveness
Addictive
behaviors
Wrong application
of force, aggression

The Devil R
Freedom from
fears or addiction
Ability to unlock
own chains
A burden lifted

The Tower
Rude awakening,
unexpected change
Collapse of a
faulty foundation
Reevaluation of
values

The Tower R
Renewed faith after
difficult life change
Pay attention to
intuitive nudges
Feeling stuck

The Star
A faith in love
Optimism, hope,
and inspiration
Abundance

The Star R
Insecurity
Loss of hope,
pessimism
Health issues

The Moon
Emotions at
full force
A reminder to
trust your psychic
intuition
New turn of
events

The Moon R
Understanding
after confusion
Clarity of light
after darkness
Relief after worry

*The Sun
Contentment
and success
Good home life
and relationships
A good marriage;
possible pregnancy*

*The Sun R
Stuck in child-
hood memories
Crossroads at
home
Need for counsel*

*Judgement
A new under-
standing of
past lessons
"I can see clearly
now!"
An awakening to
cosmic awareness*

*Judgement R
At a crossroads
Fears holding
you back
Frustrating delays*

*The World
Positive changes
at home
Your new lifestyle
is ready!
Freedom to do as
you desire*

*The World R
Lack of vision
Frustration and
postponement
You're almost
there!*

Tarot's Minor Arcana

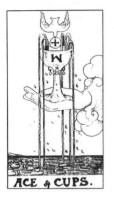

Ace of Cups
New beginnings
Opening of the
heart
Fertility and con-
ception

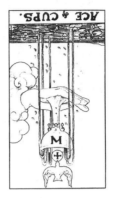

Ace of Cups R
Insecurity
Inability to con-
nect with others
Too much focus
on self

2 of Cups
Mutual emotional
understanding
Commitment
Developing bal-
anced friendship

2 of Cups R
Misunderstanding
with a loved one
Negative emotions
Lack of balance in
relationship

3 of Cups
Celebrating life
Happiness all
around
Great things
coming

3 of Cups R
Disagreements,
poor decisions
Overindulgence,
petty emotions
Need for self-
control

4 of Cups
Detachment
Need for inner,
spiritual work
Discontentment
or boredom

4 of Cups R
Ready to recon-
nect with others
Renewed activity
and ambition
Motivated to take
new direction

5 of Cups
Sorrow and loss
Need to release
emotions
Regrets, broken
dreams

5 of Cups R
Return of hope,
happiness
Renewing family
relationships
Knowledge
gained through
sorrow

6 of Cups
Family reunion
Siblings and
family values
Happy memories

6 of Cups R
Unhappy memories
Living in the past
Disappointment
with family

7 of Cups
Too *many choices!*
Preferring dreams
over reality
Indecisiveness

7 of Cups R
A decision has
been made
Renewing family
ties
You finally took
action!

8 of Cups
Desire for a
higher calling
Leaving the past
behind
Dissatisfaction
with current
lifestyle

8 of Cups R
Desire for the
material world
Renewed family
connections
Taking pleasure
in life's good
things

9 of Cups
Happy days are
here!
Your wish
fulfilled
Material success

9 of Cups R
Expecting too much
Wishes postponed
A need to develop
patience

*10 of Cups
Family harmony
and joy
Happily ever after!
Marriage or family
reunion*

*10 of Cups R
Delays in family
fulfillment
Family disagreements
Physical damage to
home*

*Page of Cups
Happiness in
family, birth
of a child
Devoted friends
and family
Positive, joyful
energy*

*Page of Cups R
Postponements
and delays
Withdrawn emotions
Oversensitive child*

*Knight of Cups
Emotional
learning
Relationship
adventure
Action toward
developing rela-
tionship*

*Knight of Cups R
Turbulent emotions
Weariness and
hesitance
Fear of commit-
ment*

Queen of Cups
Nurturing mother
figure
A focus on sensi-
tivity and intuition
Someone with
great empathy

Queen of Cups R
Emotional out-
bursts or instability
A worrier; an over-
active imagination
Take a breather!

King of Cups
Devotion, intro-
spection
Someone who
understands
others
A desire to help
others

King of Cups R
Emotional
upheaval or loss
Emotional
detachment
Turbulence in
family life

Ace of Pentacles
Focus on good
home environment
Good common
sense
Happiness of solid
foundation

Ace of Pentacles R
Frustration and
delays
Need to hold tight
to what you have
Need to reassess
priorities

2 of Pentacles
*Juggling more
than one thing
Confidence despite
stress
Balance is essential*

2 of Pentacles R
*A hard time decid-
ing something
Need to simplify;
let something go
Need for caution*

3 of Pentacles
*A time to learn
new things
Approval for
work and talent
Material gain and
success*

3 of Pentacles R
*The reality
doesn't look like
the plan
Contract dis-
agreements
Sloppy workman-
ship*

4 of Pentacles
*Holding tight to
what you have
Conservative
about money
Solid foundations*

4 of Pentacles R
*Spending more
than you have
Delay in financial
security
Generous; over-
generous*

5 of Pentacles
A deep sense of
personal loss
Feelings of
separation
Fear of abandon-
ment

5 of Pentacles R
Renewed hope
and courage
Negative cycle ends
Can now reap what
was sown

6 of Pentacles
Happy partner-
ship
Sharing with
others
Financial reward;
a new job

6 of Pentacles R
Financial disap-
pointment
More giving
than taking
Unfair, unethical
treatment

7 of Pentacles
Reaping the
rewards of
hard work
Payment for
your skill
Financial inde-
pendence

7 of Pentacles R
Poor speculation
Problems with
land or real estate
A need for caution
when speculating

8 of Pentacles
Social approval
Development of
greater skill
Recognition for
job well done

8 of Pentacles R
Delayed production
Lack of balance in
personal life
Time for a new job

9 of Pentacles
The comforts
of home
Self-sufficiency
and independence
Prosperity to
share

9 of Pentacles R
Financial insecurity
Anxiety at home
Uncertainty about
future

10 of Pentacles
The height of
family stability
Multigenerational
security
A stable and
secure maturity

10 of Pentacles R
Family feud!
Family wealth
at risk
Be cautious with
investments

*Page of Pentacles
An eager learner
A message of
happiness
Good news; good
results*

*Page of Pentacles R
A selfish or demand-
ing child or person
Delays in good news
Prejudice or rebellion*

*Knight of Pentacles
Slow and steady
wins the race
Development of
prosperous future
Wise counsel and
good stewardship*

*Knight of Pentacles R
Discontent with
present work
Absent Father figure
Irresponsibility,
slowed progress*

*Queen of Pentacles
Abundance,
productivity
The Earth Mother
personified
Positive, nurturing
person*

*Queen of Pentacles R
Financial insecurity
A lack of confidence
and trust
Losses in the home*

King of Pentacles
A good parent
figure
Assured prosperity
Someone who will
share the wealth

King of Pentacles R
Laziness or lack
of motivation
Ill-equipped for
financial success
Disorganization,
discontent about
money

Ace of Swords
A new situation
or a new child
A new way of
communicating
Feeling powerful

Ace of Swords R
The need to be cau-
tious and vigilant
Beware of aggres-
sion or force
Listen before acting

2 of Swords
Disconnected
from emotions
Indecision or
stalemate
Need to concen-
trate and focus

2 of Swords R
Remember to con-
nect to intuition
Decision has
been made
Confident action

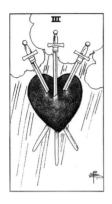

3 of Swords
Heartbreak and
sorrow
Pain, loss, and
grief
Learning about
loss and sadness

3 of Swords R
Passing sadness
Dissatisfaction,
but all is not lost
A different result
than what was
expected

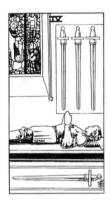

4 of Swords
R&R required!
Need for retreat
and meditation
Inner work
being done

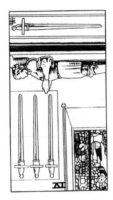

4 of Swords R
Renewed energy
Ready to fight
for own rights
Opportunity to
change existing
condition

5 of Swords
Lack of sensitiv-
ity and concern
Someone taking
unfair advantage
Destructive
behavior

5 of Swords R
Feeling too weak
to fight for others
Gossip
Desire to create
conflict

6 of Swords
Healing after
family loss
Acceptance of bet-
ter things to come
Leaving sorrows
and regrets behind

6 of Swords R
Stuck in a diffi-
cult situation
Better to wait
and see
Delays

7 of Swords
Someone's being
sneaky
A need for the
truth to come out
Unreliability and
duality

7 of Swords R
Wise counsel
will return
What was hidden
will be revealed
Freedom to move
on

8 of Swords
Self-bound to fears
Inaction, indecision
Need for good
counsel

8 of Swords R
Letting go of fear
Facing one's own
restrictions
Hope returns

*9 of Swords
Grief, sadness,
and sleeplessness
Learning to deal
with loss and
regret
Emotional
depression*

*9 of Swords R
The nightmare
is over
Negative energy is
dissipating now
New strength fol-
lowing adversity*

*10 of Swords
End of a karmic
pattern
End of a difficult
relationship
Deep sense of
loss or separation*

*10 of Swords R
Releasing of a
karmic debt
Prepared to move
ahead
Health improve-
ment*

*Page of Swords
Courage when
needed most
Using common-
sense approach
Pay attention to
details*

*Page of Swords R
Overly emotional
communication
Need to speak
mind
Importance of
truth*

Knight of Swords
Sudden change
of direction
Direct honesty,
sometimes too
direct
Awakening to
truth

Knight of Swords R
Out of control!
Arguments and dis-
ruptive behavior
Lack of emotional
insight or stamina

Queen of Swords
Ability to get to
heart of matter
Woman of strong
character
Honesty and
forthrightness

Queen of Swords R
Overly critical
person
Anxiety and mis-
communication
Judgmental or con-
tentious behavior

King of Swords
Logical analysis
Ability to probe
beneath surface
Rational counsel

King of Swords R
Self-absorption
Stubbornness and
unfair judgment
Mental exhaus-
tion

Ace of Wands
A fresh start
The first step
toward creating
your passion
A new relation-
ship or a new
baby

Ace of Wands R
Lack of motivation
Delays or
frustration
Need to regroup
and start again

2 of Wands
Waiting for results
A good
perspective
A positive attitude

2 of Wands R
Lack of follow-
through
Delays because
of others
Rethink your plan

3 of Wands
Cooperation and
partnership
Good results
forthcoming
Help from others

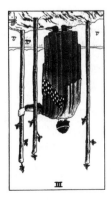

3 of Wands R
Wasted energy
Inadequate
resources
No one in the
lead

4 of Wands
Family
celebration
Contented
home life
A dream come
true

4 of Wands R
Appreciating life's
little joys
Thankfulness
Enjoyment of
small pleasures

5 of Wands
Competition
or struggles
Disagreement
and crossed
purposes
Need for clarity

5 of Wands R
Problem-solving
and harmony
Negotiation and
constructive talks
Exciting new
opportunities

6 of Wands
Family reunion
Improved rela-
tionships
Good news

6 of Wands R
Stressful conditions
Delayed journey
Develop patience;
wait it out

7 of Wands
Inner strength
and stamina
A good offense is
the best defense
Need to face
fears and turn
them around

7 of Wands R
The storm is
passing
A sense of personal
empowerment
Progress toward
goals

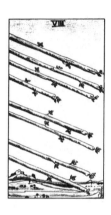

8 of Wands
Success with
goals and
relationships
Happiness and
progress
Goals within
reach

8 of Wands R
Family disagreement
and discontent
Jealousy or anger
Reorganize toward
your goal

9 of Wands
Safeguarding
the family
Prepared to
protect family,
handle adversity
Wisdom from
experience

9 of Wands R
Vulnerable
and tired
Desire to be
left alone
Anxiety and poor
health

10 of Wands
Helping too many
others at once
Stressful condi-
tions at home
Overwhelming
physical and men-
tal obligations

10 of Wands R
The burden
is lifted
Learning to
delegate
Taking the right
approach to
responsibility

Page of Wands
A message of
good news
A child or a
new child
Enthusiasm
for life

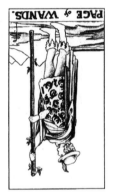

Page of Wands R
Disappointing
news
Delay in receiving
expected infor-
mation
A preoccupied
young person

Knight of Wands
Enthusiasm and
renewed energy
A new adventure
A generous loved
one

Knight of Wands R
Postponed journey
Disorganization
and chaos
An unstable person

Queen of Wands
In command of
domestic life
Someone who
encourages others'
self-sufficiency
Feminine
ambition

Queen of Wands R
Discomfort on
the home front
Immature or domi-
neering behavior
Confusion and
obstinacy

King of Wands
Someone willing
to lend a helping
hand
A good man to
have around in
a crisis
A passionate
mentor or proud
Father

King of Wands R
Lack of confidence
and focus
Feeling grumpy
and detached
Pessimism or
doubt

About the Authors

Arlene Tognetti grew up in a home where religion and spiritual ideas came together. Her mother, a traditional Catholic, and her father, a more Edgar Cayce–type individual, helped her to understand that there's more to this world than what's obvious. Arlene began studying the Tarot and Astrology in the 1970s and started her own practice in 1980. She began teaching the Tarot at the University of Washington in the Experimental College in 1982, and currently teaches the Tarot at Pierce College in Tacoma. Arlene's focus is on enlightening her students and clients: "I want everyone to learn what Tarot, Astrology, and Psychic Intuition are all about and how these Intuitive Arts can help them grow and look at the choices and alternatives in their lives." Arlene is expert author, with Lisa Lenard, of *The Complete Idiot's Guide to Tarot, Second Edition.* Arlene lives in the Seattle area. Her website is www.mellinetti.com.

Cathy Jewell is a writer and editor who lives happily with her family in Silver Spring, Maryland.

Amaranth Illuminare is a leading book producer, developing New Age and holistic wellness books for mainstream readers. Amaranth's goal: Touch readers' lives. In addition to *The Intuitive Arts* series, Amaranth has developed many books, including *Empowering Your Life with Joy* by Gary McClain, Ph.D., and Eve Adamson; *Thyroid Balance* by Glenn Rothfeld, M.D., and Deborah S. Romaine; and *Menu for Life: African Americans Get Healthy, Eat Well, Lose Weight, and Live Beautifully* by Otelio Randall, M.D., and Donna Randall. Amaranth's founder and creative director, Lee Ann Chearney, is the author of *Visits: Caring for an Aging Parent* and editor of *The Quotable Angel.*

The Intuitive Arts series

Use Astrology, Tarot, and Psychic Intuition to See Your Future

Discover how you can combine the Intuitive Arts to find answers to questions of daily living, use tools to help you see and make changes in your future, claim your brightest destiny, and fulfill your essential nature.

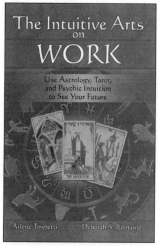

1-59257-108-5

ISBN: 1-59257-106-9

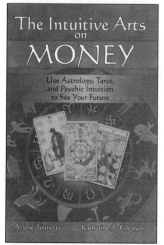

ISBN: 1-59257-107-7

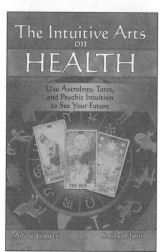

ISBN: 1-59257-109-3

ALPHA
A member of Penguin Group (USA) Inc.